Small Beginnings

The Photographic Journey
Through the Life of Merze Tate

SEASON Press LLC

Little Merze
had no idea
What her life
would bring,
When she
posed for the
camera,
With her mom
and siblings.

STATE OF MICHIGAN,)
County of Isabella) ss.
Mt. Pleasant, Michigan)

CERTIFIED COPY OF RECORD OF BIRTH

I, MAYNARD S. GILMORE, Clerk of the County of Isabella, and of the Circuit Court thereof, the same being a Court of Record having a Seal, do hereby certify that the following is a copy of the Record of Birth of

VERNIE MERZE TATE _____ now remaining in my office, and of the whole thereof, viz:

CHILD

| SURNAME AND CHRISTIAN NAME, IF ONE BE GIVEN | | | DATE OF BIRTH | | | SEX |
FIRST	MIDDLE	LAST	MONTH	DAY	YEAR	
VERNIE	MERZE	TATE	FEB	6	1905	White Female
COUNTY	BIRTH PLACE CITY, TOWN OR LOCATION		LOCAL FILE NO.		BIRTH NO.	
ISABELLA	ROLLAND		L-4 XP-220		247	

PARENTS

	BIRTH PLACE OF EACH
MOTHER—MAIDEN NAME MYRTLE KATORA LETT	MICHIGAN
FATHER—NAME CHAS. TATE	OHIO

Date of Record JUNE 14, 1906

In Testimony Whereof, I have hereunto set my hand and affixed the seal of said Circuit Court,

the ___2nd___ day of ___Feb.___ A. D. 19 70

MAYNARD S. GILMORE _____ Clerk.

MAYNARD S. GILMORE

By _Katherine O. Donnell_ Deputy Clerk.

FORM No. M-800 DOUBLEDAY BROS. & CO. KALAMAZOO, MICH. 517589

Myrtle Tate went into labor during a snowstorm in 1906. The doctor could not make it to the home, so the neighbor, Vernie Finch, came to the rescue. Because her help, Myrtle named her daughter, Vernie. She gave her the middle name Merze, based on a character from a book she admired. The birth certificate notes the baby was White! Older half-siblings Theo, Hershel, and Thelma Cross stand here with Merze and her baby brother Keith.

Her family had been pioneers,
Who blazed a trail so true.
They were soldiers, farmers, abolitionists,
And inventor of the first clock
Benjamin Banneker, too!

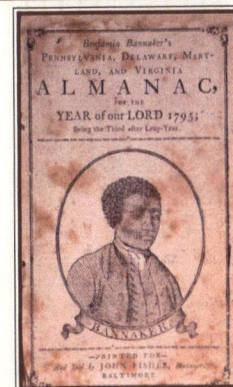

Merze is a descendent of the Lett and Tate families. Pioneers John Tate and Sara (Guy) were among the first African American settlers in Mecosta County, Michigan; Aquilla Lett was an abolitionist and Civil War soldier; Merze's cousin Claude Guy and half-brother Herschel Cross, pose in their Navy uniforms during World War I; Settlers from the family pose with their livestock. Benjamin Banneker (from the Lett family line) was an inventor, mathematician, and scientist. He created the first clock in America.

Merze wanted to see the world
They knew she could not stay.
She had to leave everyone she
knew, To find a different way.

Family members say Merze was never without her camera. During one of her last summer visits home, she took photos of everyone she knew. She placed the photos in a scrapbook she cherished for the rest of her life.

1925

1926

GRADING STREETS BLANCHARD MICH.

A one-room schoolhouse was the place
Where she began to see,
To make a dream reality,
Education is the key.

Merze poses with other classmates from her country schoolhouse. Her brother Keith poses next to the class sign.

Merze poses with her classmates at Blanchard High School. She was in the 10th grade and the youngest in the class when named the valedictorian. The school burned down that year and the temporary facility did not have the room to hold the science and other courses needed to qualify for college.

What would she do?

High School, Battle Creek, Mich

State Normal School, Kalamazoo, Mich

Blanchard Negress Is Best Student in Kalamazoo Normal

Kalamazoo, Jan. 10.—Merze Tate, Negress, working her way through Western State Normal and carrying extra classes to complete a four-year course in three years, won the highest scholastic honors from a student body of 2,300 the first term this year, it has been announced by Registrar John C. Hoekje.

Miss Tate received all A's in six courses. She is a graduate of Battle Creek high school and lives at Blanchard in Isabella county. Next June she is to get her A. B. degree.

On her pathway as a scholar
She earned degrees and Ph.D.s,
And became the first black graduate
Of Oxford University.

1925 Western Graduate Was Honored at Oxford

Miss Merze Tate, Who Has Her A.B. From Western State, Is Among the Oxford Grads

The following clipping regarding Miss Marze Tate, now of Detroit, a graduate of Western State Teachers College in 192', will be of extreme interest to those who knew her and should prove of interest to other students.

Miss Merze Tate, formerly instructor of history at the Crispus Attucks High School, Indianapolis, has just crowned her already brilliant achievements as teacher and scholar with another laurel: the winning of the B. Litt. (degree which ranks with our Ph.D.) from the ancient and historic Oxford University. The degree was awarded on the basis of a two year's research into the "Movement for Disarmament 1853-1914," research which was done under the personal direction of A. E. Zimmern, Montague Burton, Professor of International Relations and advisor to the British Cabinet.

Merze completed 11th and 12th grades at Battle Creek Central High School (1922) with all A's. She graduated from Western State Teacher's College in 1927 (Western Michigan University) with the school record of 45 A's and 6 B's; and earned the four-year degree in three years. Merze completed a master's degree at Columbia University in 1930.

As member of Alpha Kappa Alpha Sorority, Merze earned their third Foreign Fellow award of $1,000, which the organization doubled when they learned she would use it toward her study at Oxford University where she would become the first African American graduate (1935). She earned another mark in history in 1941 as the first African American female to earn a Ph.D. in Political Science from Radcliffe College at Harvard University.

Respected by educators,
And Department of the State
The military honored her
For helping Integrate.

Jim Crow laws kept Merze Tate from teaching high school in Michigan. In 1927, with the help of President Dwight Waldo of Western State Teacher's College (now Western Michigan University), she was hired at Crispus Attucks High School in Indianapolis, Indiana. The history teacher started a Travel Club where dozens of students visited such places as Washington D.C., Pennsylvania, and Niagara Falls!

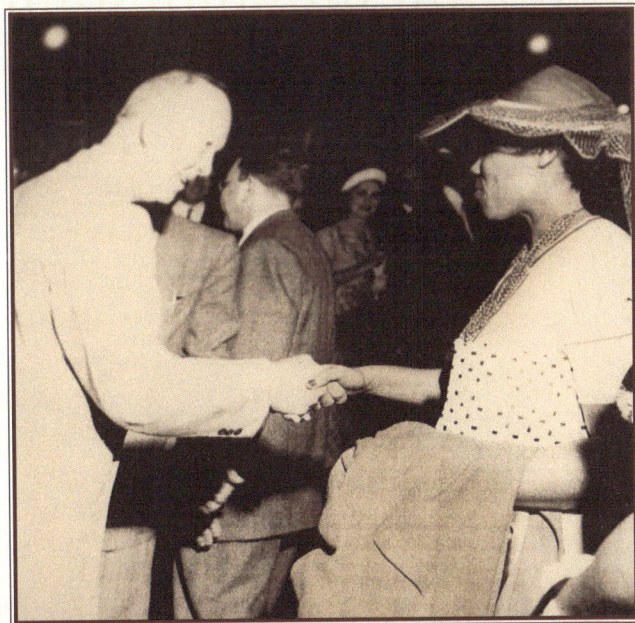

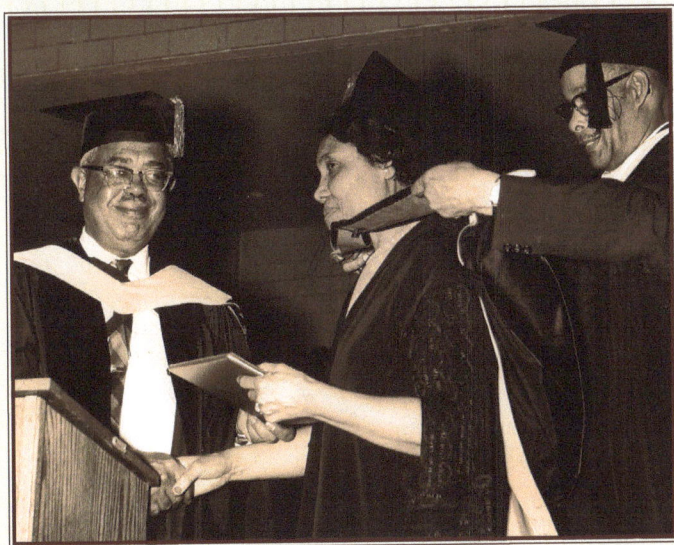

Merze Tate was an expert on atomic energy. In 1948 she represented the Department of State with General Dwight Eisenhower during the United Nations Educational Scientific and Cultural Organization(UNESCO) conference. She was one of three Americans (and the only African American) invited to participate.

A military unit in Germany honored her after an article she published in the Afro-American newspaper uncovered segregation in their units. Western Michigan University and Morgan State College celebrated her with honorary doctorate degrees.

History came to life
When she traveled to faraway places.
The people she met around the world
Had some of the most friendly faces!

Merze longed to see the ancient ruins and experience the world she learned about in her history books. She traveled around the world twice and made many friends along the way.

Playing Indian

As Fulbright Scholar in India,
She met their first Prime Minister.
The culture, beauty, and history
Was something she would always remember.

Merze was the first African American Fulbright Scholar in India (1950). She taught at the university, and captured their culture on film—even a man who ran on hot coals! She used her Press card from the Afro-American newspaper to have access to Prime Minister Jawaharlal Nehru to create a photo story.

They posed for her camera,
No need for translation.
A child's smile is the same
in every single nation.

Whether she was in Denmark, Hawaii, or Calcutta, children gravitated to Merze and her camera.

She ventured to the Taj Mahal,
And even drove through a Redwood tree.
She rode a camel in Egypt,
Stood on lava in Hawaii.

Merze had adventures from California to Cairo. Wherever she went, she always learned something new...even how to ride a bike while in England!

Professor, author, historian,
And master of many tasks.
Inventor, photographer, philanthropist,
Her mark on this world would last.

July 27, 1948.   M. TATE   2,446,066

MIXING UNIT FOR REFRIGERATORS

Filed Dec. 23, 1943   2 Sheets—Sheet 1

Inventor
Merze Tate
By S. F. Randolph
Attorney

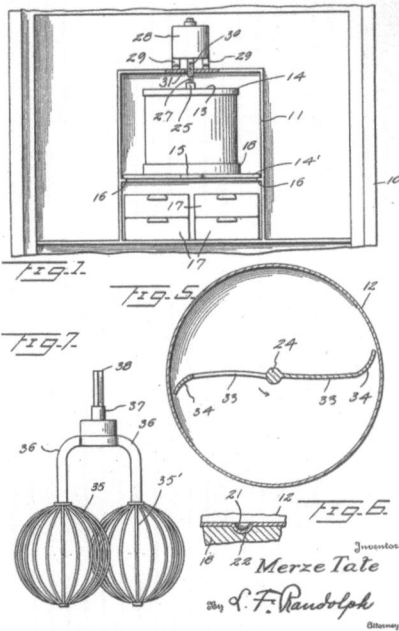

Merze wrote five books and dozens of articles on international political issues for major universities. Her ties to Western Michigan, Radcliffe, and Howard universities led her to leave millions in financial contributions that would help students for years to come. The Merze Tate Center in Sangren Hall at WMU was funded through her efforts.

Like her ancestor, Benjamin Banneker, she too was an inventor! Her patent for an ice cream-making process used by major appliance companies.

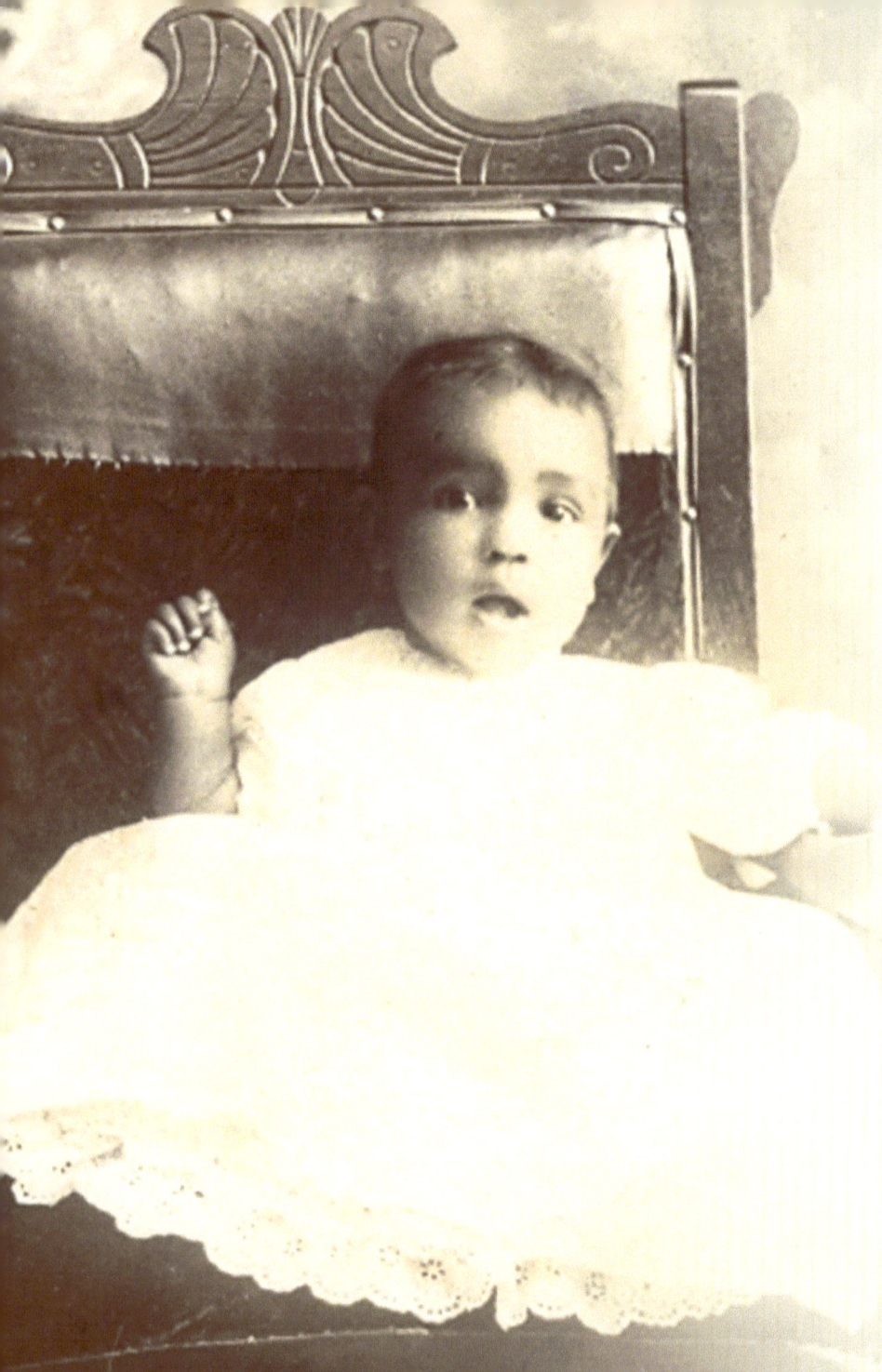

When you
step out,
To explore life's
possibilities,
You too, can
be an example,
Of what
can come
From Small
Beginnings.

Merze poses in her baby gown, and later the graduation cap and gown of Oxford University. She wrote the poem, "Thoughts on Entering Oxford," on the ocean liner headed to Oxford University in 1932.

Thoughts on Entering Oxford

When I consider what before me lies,
A chance to make a name, a chance to die,
A chance to gather from these ancient walls
Covered with ivy, hiding famous halls.
What this Mother of Learning is
ready to bestow
On one who has the courage
and strength to go
Through endless hours of toil
and grief and joy.
I think of constant strife without these walls
And wonder if our lives are worth the while
We spend on earth nurturing petty wiles:
Then I recall: "Who best bare His mild yoke
they serve Him best."
This relieves my mind, and then I rest.
And make my one big wish a prayer to be
A credit to my race and my Sorority.

Merze Tate Explorers
Est. 2008

Merze Tate taught at Crispus Attucks High School in Indianapolis, Indiana from 1927 to 1932. As a History teacher, Merze wanted to introduce her students to the world she taught them each day. She started a Travel Club, and on Easter Sunday, 1932, was the sponsor of 40 students who took the train to Washington D.C. The Indianapolis newspaper noted they were the "first colored students to Washington D.C. west of the Appalachian". Before she left for Oxford University in 1932, Tate later took 100 students to Niagara Falls.

Sonya Hollins became fascinated with Tate's life as she researched her for an article. The photograph in the scrapbooks Tate left to Western Michigan University were captivating; particularly one featuring the girls in her Travel Club. Hollins was led to start her own version of Tate's Travel Club in 2008 with 12 girls in grades 6-12th.

Today, the Merze Tate Explorers is a Non-profit Organization for girls in grades 4th-12th with an interest in career exploration and travel through media. The students have traveled the world and have met women who head corporations, and those of national and international acclaim, who they interview for their annual magazine, Girls Can! Many of the charter members have gone on to graduate from college and lives which mirror some of Tate's academic and professional accomplishments.

For more information on the Merze Tate Explorers, visit: www.merzetate.com.

The girls of Merze Tate's Travel Club of 1932 are the inspiration for today's Merze Tate Explorers. Above: 2009 at Kalamazoo Valley Museum; 2010 at East Hall on the campus of Western Michigan University where Merze Tate attended classes; 2017 in Battle Creek as the Explorers received the Sojourner Truth Institute's 1st Velma Laws-Clay Vanguard Award.

Abbreviated History of Merze Tate

1905- Born Vernie Merze Tate in Blanchard, Michigan

1920- Graduates from 10th grade in Blanchard; named valedictorian.

1921-Enters Battle Creek Central High School; wins Hinman Oratorical Contest.

1922- Graduates with all A's from Battle Creek Central, Battle Creek, Michigan.

1927- Earns a bachelor's degree in three years from Western State Teacher's College (now Western Michigan University), Kalamazoo, Michigan; graduated with the school's highest academic record of 45 A's and 6 B's.

1927-32- Works as history teacher at Crispus Attucks High School in Indianapolis, Indiana.; Starts school Travel Club and takes students to Washington D.C., Pennsylvania, Niagara Falls.

1930- Earns master's degree in European History from Columbia University.

1935- Becomes the first African American to earn a B. Litt degree from Oxford University in England; Dean of Women, Barber-Scotia College, North Carolina; studies at University of Berlin, Germany.

1936- Chair of Social Sciences of Bennett College.

1941- First African American female to earn a Ph.D. in Political Science from Harvard University's Radcliffe College, inducted into Phi Beta Kappa, inducted into Pi Gamma Mu (National Social Science Honor Society); Dean/Professor of Political Science at Morgan State University.

1942- Completes her book, *The Disarmament Illusion: The Movement for a Limitation of Armaments to 1907* (Macmillan Press). Hired as first female History professor at Howard University, Washington D.C.

1943- Filed for a patent for a mixing unit for making ice cream in the freezer.

1948- One of three Americans and only African American representative at UNESCO (United Nations Educational, Scientific, and Cultural Organization); receives Honorary Doctorate of Letters from Western Michigan University; authored *The United States and Armaments* (Harvard University Press).

1950- Fulbright Scholar in India and completes 44,000 mile trip around the world.

1954- Harvard University's Radcliffe College presents Tate with Alumna Award (the first African American to receive the honor).

1962- Cinematographer for U.S. State Department.

1965- Author of *The United States and the Hawaiian Kingdom* (Yale University Press) became one of the world's leading experts on Hawaii.

1968- Author of *Hawaii: Reciprocity or Annexation* (Michigan State University Press).
1970- First African American female to earn the Distinguished Alumni Award from Western Michigan University.

1973-76- Guest of largest mining company in Liberia, LAMC's guest of Foreign Affairs Dept. in Rhodesia, guest of Iron and Steel Corp. of South Africa; author of Diplomacy in the Pacific: A Collection of Twenty-Seven Articles on Diplomacy in the Pacific and Influence of the Sandwich (Hawaiian) Islands Missionaries.

1977- Completes her second trip around the world; retires from Howard University.

1980- Donates $50,000 to WMU; Distinguished Alumnus Award of American Association of State Colleges and Universities

1984- Contributes $150,000 to WMU to create the Tate Center, Computer Information Center, and established scholarship.

1990- Donates $1 million to WMU student academic endowment; featured in *Jet* Magazine.

1996- Dies of a heart attack in her home in Washington D.C. and leaves a legacy to universities which played a role in her successes.

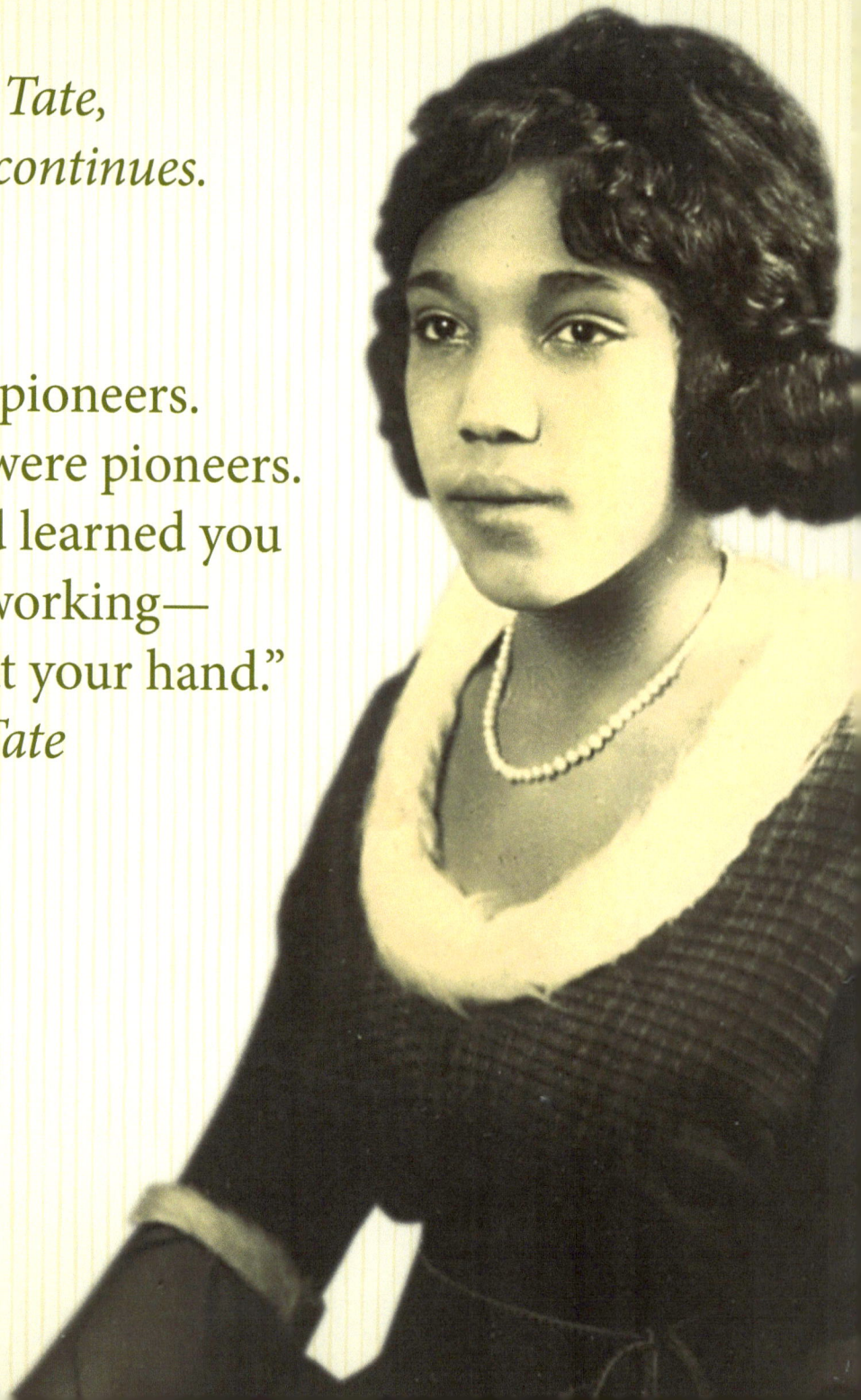

To Merze Tate,
Whose legacy continues.

"I came from pioneers.
My grandparents were pioneers.
They worked, and learned you
get things by working—
not by holding out your hand."
Merze Tate

Photographs* and articles are from the scrapbooks of Merze Tate located in the Zhang Legacy Collection Center, Archives and Regional History Collection located on the campus of Western Michigan University, Kalamazoo, MI.

*Photographs on pages 4, 5 are courtesy of Marsha Todd-Stewart, curator of www.oldsettlersreunion.com
Poem, "Thoughts on Entering Oxford," taken from *Professor Merze Tate: A Profile-1905-1996* by Joseph E. Harris, *Negro History Bulletin* July-Dec., 1998.

Special thanks to Sharon Carlson, Professor of University Libraries, Zhang Legacy Center, Archives and Regional History Collections Director at Western Michigan University who has been a valuable resource for this project. Very special thanks to my family who worked as a team to make this book possible.

Season Press LLC/Community Voices
P.O. Box 51042
Kalamazoo, MI 49001
Ordering Information:
Quantity sales. Special discounts are available on quantity purchases by non-profit organizations, corporations, and others. For details, contact the publisher at the address above.
Orders by U.S. trade bookstores and wholesalers. Please contact Ingram Spark at: www.ingramspark.com

Published in collaboration with Season Press LLC
Design and Layout by Sean Hollins/Fortitude Graphic Design and Printing
Publisher's Cataloging-in-Publication data
Hollins, Sonya.
Small Beginnings: The Photographic Journey Through the Life of Merze Tate / Sonya Bernard-Hollins
p. cm.
Library of Congress Control Number: 2018940345
ISBN 13: 978-0-9991334-7-7
1. Merze Tate —Biography—Juvenile Literature. 2. African American History —Michigan.
3. Photography—Travel—Juvenile literature

COMMUNITY VOICES

A Community Voices Imprint
First Edition
10 9 8 7 6 5 4 3 2 1
Printed in the United States of America

www.ingramcontent.com/pod-product-compliance
Lightning Source LLC
Chambersburg PA
CBHW042026090426
42811CB00016B/1753